Written By: Krystle Flynn
Illustrated By: Erika Busse

Scan this QR Code to receive a printable version of ABC Yogi!

www.theabcyogi.com

Copyright © 2021 by Krystle Flynn

All rights reserved. No part of this book may be reproduced or used in any manner without written permission of the copyright owner except for the use of quotations in a book review.

ISBN: 9781736398104

For Lily, who filled in all the empty spaces
& for Luke, for always holding its container.

◎

A special thank you to my forever family, yoga pals, & true friends, Suzanne, Sandi, Daphne, Stephanie, Laura, Liz, Margaret, Chip, Nico, Angela, Jennifer, Jamie, Sarah, & Shawn.

◎

And to my illustrator Erika — thank you for making the dreams in my head something that could actually be seen by others in such a beautiful way.

◎

Thank you all from the entirety of my heart.

−Crystal clear thoughts−
−Kind and unique expressions−
−& Endless compassion for oneself & all of those around you−
Namaste
Krystle

Feel your feet soft atop the moss,
Your wings float up, as you begin to soar across

DOWNWARD DOG

Upside down, hands and feet
plant in the ground,
Feel your body light and sound

One knee on the ground
Opposite foot pressing down
One arm stretches over
Imagine your heart open like a four leaf clover!

HALF MOON
(modified)

Lift one leg into the air
Heart opens towards the moon
Lungs fill up,
just like a balloon

RAINBOW

Sitting with legs crossed,
One on top of the other
Arms draw overhead,
Painting the sky with colors

UNICORN

Shine your light
With your hand as a horn
Transform into a magical unicorn

GLOSSARY

ENGLISH	SANSKRIT (pronunciation)
Airplane or Warrior III	Virabhadrasana III (veer-uh-buh-DRAHS-uh-nuh)
Bow	Dhanurasana (DHAN-yoor-AHS-uh-nuh)
Cobra	Bhujangasana (Boo-JANG-ahs-uh-nuh)
Downward Dog	Adho Mukha Svanasana (AH-doh MOO-kah- shvah-NAHS-uh-nuh)
Elephant or Forward Fold	Uttanasana (OOT-ah-NAHS-uh-nuh)
Frog	Mandukasana (man-doo-KAHS-uh-nuh)
Gate Latch	Parighasana (par-ee-GOSS-uh-nuh)
Half Moon (modified)	Ardha Chandrasana (ARD-uh chan-DRAHS-uh-nuh)
Ice Block of Knees to Chest	Apanasana (ah-PAH-NAH-suh-nuh)
Jack in the Box or Modified Knees to Chest	Apanasana (ah-PAH-NAH-suh-nuh)
Kangaroo or Chair (modified)	Utkatasana (OOT-kuh-TAHS-uh-nuh)
Lion	Simhasana (sim-HASS-uh-nuh)
Mountain	Tadasana (tah-DAHS-uh-nuh)
Narwhal or Grasshopper (modified)	Salabhasana (shal-ab-AHS-uh-nuh)
Oyster or Bound Angle	Baddha Konasana (BAH-duh cone-AHS-uh-nuh)
Pretzel or Half Lord of the Fishes	Ardha Matsyendrasana (ARD-uh MAHT-see-ehn-DRAHS-uh-nuh)
Queen or Easy Seated (modified)	Sukhasana (soo-KAHS-uh-nuh)
School Bus or Seated Forward Fold	Paschimottanasana pah-chee-moe-TAH-NAHS-uh-nuh)
Table Top	Bharmanasana (bar-mahn-AHS-uh-nuh)
Unicorn or Warrior I	Virabhadrasana I (veer-uh-buh-DRAHS-uh-nuh)
Volcano or Forward Fold	Urdhva Hastasana (OORD-vah has-tas-uh-nuh)
Wheel	Urdhva Dhanurasana (OORD-vah don-yoor-AHS-uh-nuh)
Xylophone or Upward Facing Plank	Purvottanasana (PUR-voh-tun-AHS- uh-nuh
Yoga breath or Upward Salute (modified)	Urdhva Hastasana (OORD-vah has-tas-uh-nuh)
Zen or Corpse	Savasana (sha-VAH-suh- nuh)

www.ingramcontent.com/pod-product-compliance
Lightning Source LLC
Chambersburg PA
CBHW040109120526
44589CB00040B/2830